MW01709852

TAURUS
Thru the Numbers

Paul & Valeta Rice

SAMUEL WEISER, INC.
York Beach, Maine 03910

First published in 1983 by
Samuel Weiser, Inc.
Box 612
York Beach, Maine 03910

Second printing, 1988

ISBN 0-87728-566-7 (Taurus)

Library of Congress Catalog Card Number: 82-63004

Printed in the United States of America
by Mitchell-Shear, Inc.

Contents

AUTHORS

If Valeta and Paul Rice sound familiar, it may be because of their extensive travel to many cities from Fairbanks, Alaska, down the coast of California and across the continental United States to Baltimore, Maryland. During their invitational stopovers, they conduct workshops and seminars about Name Analysis and Birth Analysis. They have been traveling together and teaching for over twenty years.

While their professions are different (Valeta is a minister and psychic counselor, Paul is an engineer), they have been interested in occult studies for more than forty years, starting with their introduction to a book about ESP from Duke University. Their search for esoteric knowledge carried them into astrology, reincarnation, palmistry, tarot, color, music, I Ching, ESP, dream analysis, the qabala, yoga, structural dynamics, meditation/visualization/healing and many more sciences. Their Socratic and regression techniques have been rewarding to clients.

Their newest book, *Potential: The Name Analysis Book*, also published by Samuel Weiser, Inc., provides an in-depth look at the special numerological nuances your name holds. Learn about your desire self, your dormant self, your special abilities number—even your karmic numbers and what you need to work on in this lifetime! *Potential* is a book to show you "what's in a name," and if you wish, show you how to change it!

The authors are available for private consultation and for lectures. Interested readers should contact them at:

Paul and Valeta Rice
F.A.C.E. Association
177 Webster Street, #A105
Monterey, CA 93940

WHEN?

When shall I start my next project?
When should I ask for a raise?
When should I sign that contract?
When should I get married?
How will I feel when I retire?

How many times has a person looked for an answer to these questions? During this modern age the veil has been lifted on the ancient science of the vibration of the NUMBERS. This ancient science, known as the *metaphysical science of numerology,* was developed by Pythagoras, who lived in the sixth century B.C.

The simplicity of NUMEROLOGY is astounding. If you can count on your fingers you can use Numerology. It requires only a few hours study before you can begin to put to use the basic facts that you have acquired. This knowledge will give one the opportunity to see himself and other acquaintances in a better light. Apparently its simplicity is the reason Numerology was used less than other occult sciences in the past, and our society today seems to prefer complexity also.

Surprisingly, the knowledge of the numbers which govern your life will reveal many things you already know, that you had suspected or you had hoped were true.

The Numerologist takes his place alongside the Astrologer, Graphologist, Palmist and the Tarot reader, who all believe that we came into this life, not by chance, but by choice, and from these arts or sciences much can be revealed about a person's life.

Numerology reveals the vibrations in many categories including the number connected to the Birth Date, the Personal Year, the Personal Month and how the planet vibrations correlate to these numbers.

The awareness of the numbers connected to these categories helps us with a yearly and monthly course to follow.

Everyone wants to be happy and prosperous. Many unfortunate people have not learned to harmonize their birthdate vibrations with the timing of their decisions.

We are constantly called upon to make decisions which may make significant changes in our lives. Often we make the wrong decisions over family, friends, or in business because our "TIMING" is off.

The simple system of the vibration of the numbers and how they pertain to your life and the timing of your decisions will help you to come to logically deduced insights and, if carefully followed,will make you increasingly happy and prosperous throughout your lifetime.

Pythagoras, who lived twenty-five centuries ago, is considered the Father of Numbers. It is believed that he received his knowledge of the occult value of the numbers while in Egypt and Babylon. He taught these concepts and many more in his School of Occult Philosophy where the few who were allowed to attend learned how "everything can be related to numbers."

The Science of Numerology is not a quick way to happiness and achievement; it is only by becoming aware of your favorable number vibrations and then changing the unfavorable vibrations that you can smooth your pathway.

Numbers live and numbers tell and everyone can become aware of their vibrations and their relationship to themselves through the numbers.

We have explored the mundane and esoteric values of the numbers and their relationship to astrology with a lot of help from our guides.

This knowledge we wish to share with you.

TAURUS

April 21st to May 22nd | *FIXED: EARTH*

The BULL | *Ruler: VENUS*

The Taurus person is steady and very patient although he cannot be pushed into something that he does not feel is right for him. Watch him stretch his patience if you are working for a Taurus for he can only be challenged so long; then this nice, kindly, perfectly harmless person turns into a raging bull, crashing through the china shop of your carelessness, bringing havoc when you least expect it.

You cannot command the Taurian although he/she can be led to think that "this wonderful idea" you had really comes from something he or she triggered in you. Then the direction you want to go will be the direction the Taurian wants to go.

Taurians are practical; they admire people who can discipline themselves. They are fair and recognize talent as well as recognizing the "games" you could be playing to get what you want.

Taurians are so factual and honest in their approach that few of them enter the sales field. However, there are a few customers who prefer the blunt, direct approach and will buy from none other, as the Taurian can be trusted to tell the truth.

When entering a field that is unfamiliar they need the time to adjust. Then their native intelligence will survey the needs of the job, evaluate the problems connected with it and get to work being the best darn employees you ever had as long as you can keep them busy. They like order and organization and make top managers as they will stand for no nonsense after giving the employee a fair chance to learn his job.

The love of beauty is inherent in the Taurian, love of fine fabrics, well-made furniture, a home that is well planned with coordinated colors and simplicity of design. The art objects are of first quality but useful.

Taurians are affectionate, they are passionate in their first developing encounters and this develops into a warm, loving relationship. They are ideal for marriage as they are faithful to their committed mate.

PARTNERS: A relationship with a person who has a similar number is best, i.e., a number that radiates confidence, stablility, loyalty and devotion, as these are the qualities of a Taurian. Usually Virgos or Capricorns make good mates if their numbers are compatible. Taurians are apt to get confused if their mate wants to command them or is erratic in decisions.

VENUS: This planet, the ruler of Taurus, is love energy. This artistic, refined, courteous and elegant planet of beauty and love rules the stubbornness of the BULL. The bull wants to charge ahead, getting his own way, yet the love energy modifies the frontal attack unless Taurus is pushed into a corner.

FIXED: This is a Taurus' aspect of force manifesting in matter. This is a power sign, coiled energy ready to manifest as will power. Interested in ideas and values, ready to put wants into action.

EARTH: The element of Taurus, the virtues we bring with us to assist us in this lifetime. This is the practical, patient and loving willingness to build sign which manifests as all-seeing on the highest level.

NEGATIVE VIBRATIONS: Indifference, indolence, stubbornness, jealousy and greediness. Wanting to possess material things no matter how much force is needed.

NUMBERS: The NUMBER that is connected to Taurus' BIRTH SIGN increases or decreases Taurus' energy. Wherever you have Taurus in your chart look at the influence your DESTINY NUMBER has on this house in your horoscope.

HOW TO COMPUTE YOUR DESTINY

Your DESTINY, sometimes called the LIFE PATH, is the road that you as an individual travel. This is why you are here, what you should be doing in this lifetime in order to fulfill your soul. The NUMBER combined with your TAURUS BIRTH SIGN reveals your soul urge, your reason for incarnating this lifetime. If you do not follow your DESTINY, you can become frustrated with unresolved goals.

Each month is represented by a number:

JANUARY	1	APRIL	4	JULY	7	OCTOBER	1
FEBRUARY	2	MAY	5	AUGUST	8	NOVEMBER	2
MARCH	3	JUNE	6	SEPTEMBER	9	DECEMBER	3

Write your BIRTHDATE on your PERSONAL CHART, page 26, using the NAME of your month—APRIL or MAY—not the number of the month. Be sure to use the full year, *i.e.*, 1935, *NOT* '35; or 1940, *NOT* '40, or whatever is the year of your birth. We use the "1" in the year, *i.e.*, 1935, 1966, 1940, as well as the rest of the numbers.

On scratch paper add the number of the month, the day of the month and the year of your birth together; then reduce this number by constantly adding the numbers together until you come to a single digit or a MASTER NUMBER.

The MASTER NUMBERS are **11, 22, 33, 44, 55 and 66.**

EXAMPLE:	April	27,	1953(1953 = 1 + 9 + 5 + 3 + = 18 = **9**)	
	4	9	9	= **22** also **4**
EXAMPLE:	May	5,	1932	
	5	5	6	= 16; 1 + 6 = **7**
EXAMPLE:	April	26,	1940	
	4	26	14	= **44** also **8**

Experiment with your birthdate and see if you can come up with a "hidden" MASTER NUMBER.

We call this last example *Research and Discovery* since we have found a *hidden* Master Number. When the Master Numbers are hidden an unexpected talent lies in the direction of the vibration of that particular number.

EXAMPLE: April 26, 1920 = 4 + 2 + 6 + 1 + 9 + 2 + 0 = **6**
EXAMPLE: 4 26 3 (1 + 9 + 2 + 0) = **33**

So, Taurus, every time you find a **1**, **4**, **6** or **8** in your birth sign or someone else's birth sign try all these methods. Then you find out if you or another person is vibrating on the Master Number or the single digit. There are persons who are content to vibrate and work on the single digit pulsation and put their talents to excellent use in that position rather than try for the esoteric vibration of the Master Numbers. This depends a lot on other numbers which concern several other categories in numerology.

The main purpose of finding your DESTINY NUMBER is to realize where you are in life's stream and learn to flow with it.

The DESTINY NUMBER and your BIRTH SIGN are two things that you cannot change. You were born on a certain day, month, and year, for you chose to be here at that time to experience what you have come to this lifetime to learn.

Another way to research and discover if you have a hidden Master Number is to add this way:

April 23, 1920 = 4 + 23 + 19 + 20 = **66** or **3**
May 3, 1928 = 5 + 3 + 19 + 28 = **55** or 10 or **1**
April 23, 1916 = 4 + 5 + 19 + 16 = **44** or **8**

We always like to show the single digit that belongs to the Master Number to see which level a person is on. There is a great deal more study to be done on this way to discover *where* the talent is in the birthdate.

DESTINY NUMBER 1

This pulsating creative number will release you, Taurus, from that earthbound feeling of moving slowly and deliberately. This number helps you to fly, Taurus. Your original ideas and innovative methods spiral you out of the *fixed* vibration of manifesting always on a logical plane. This does not mean that you relinquish your analytical attitude toward your life. This number gives you more freedom of expression and confidence in your own creative abilities.

Your quick mind moves faster than the average, leaving your slower-paced friends behind and sometimes in chaos as they cannot follow the different levels of creativity on which you are operating.

You already have a strong personality and are independently oriented which can be lonely for you. It is difficult for you to maneuver others, rather you expect them to go along with you and your novel ideas when you are expressing this **1** creative number.

Remember that authority needs to be delegated and not hovered over if your employees are to do their finest work. Supervision, yes; repression, no. This vibration concerns an employee as well as the boss.

There is constant optimism in communicating with your mate, lover, etc., for your creative ideas will keep the relationship going. Your mate may end up a little off balance because of your surprises!

NEGATIVE: Seek assistance once in a while when your creative juices refuse to flow—don't always be a bull-headed "Mother, I'll do it myself" kind of person. How can anyone detract from the firmly fixed, earthy Taurian who has such splendid imagination?

Number **1**

Color: Red—for energy. Project this to others. Element: Fire—more energy. Take your vitamins. Musical Note: C—the self-starter.

DESTINY NUMBER 2

This is the number of patience, Taurus, which you usually do not need, as you are long-suffering and only explode when the last straw comes wafting down to settle on your already burdened back. Then watch out! The Bull paws the ground and snorts and charges!

This is the number that is responsive to emotional appeal, the sensitive person who can see in others the need to be loved. As a **2**, whenever a person appeals to your sympathies you are apt to open your arms and embrace them and their woes with an open heart. These people with problems better be careful with you and not try to trick you or betray you. Your patience is long and you prefer peace, but you can whirl around and face them if you feel they are using you unfairly.

This sensitivity to rhythms gives you the grace to move smoothly through life, using diplomacy and counseling others with rare insight. You would never take them into never-never land as you are too down to earth, showing others the sane approach to life.

NEGATIVE: Impatience is the other side of a **2**, wanting to get the job done NOW! Overly sensitive to criticism about your work, your dress, your clothes, or your friends. You *can* turn off your feelings if you feel betrayed and will withdraw into a neutral corner to glower at your enemies. Then you can plan how to get even with a flourish!

Number **2**

Color: Orange—for balance and harmony, the vibrant color of the sun at dawn and sunset.
Element: Water—dealing in and with the emotions; soothing the fevered brow of discontent.
Musical Note: *D*—for harmony and tranquility.

DESTINY NUMBER 3

Your humor is warm and earthy, Taurus, and this life is the time to show others how charming you can be. Play a little and use your Venus ruler to bring love and light to you. Taurians don't feel that they have to chase after fun and gaiety, it will just gravitate toward them, like a moth to a flame as they (Taurians) are so *there*. Very solid folk, enjoying the antics of others, even as they sit in a corner with little to say.

Have you thought of going into drama, Taurus? Some of our most famous personalities have taken the pathway that leads to fame, like Fred Astaire, Gary Cooper, Bing Crosby, William Shakespeare, Harry S. Truman and Sigmund Freud to name just a few. Look at the common denominator of these people mentioned. They all knew what they wanted, and in one way or another were in the entertainment field—even Mr. Truman.

The **1** is the creative factor and it combines with the **2** of compassion to assist you to bring forth your talents so that the world may see them.

3 is expression and communication for you, Taurus, using your innate honesty and logic for getting your message across to others, whether it be over the footlights or across the table.

Your mate or lover may never hear flowery poetry from you, but your perseverance in love will sometimes put Scorpio to shame.

NEGATIVE: There is more chance of becoming conceited with this number, Taurus, if you become negative about yourself. You may dabble in many pursuits without any definite purpose in life. You could also become intolerant of those who do not stay with their life goals. It is good to look at where you are coming from and how to evaluate yourself and others. Are you jealous of them?

Number **3**

Color: Yellow—for expression.
Element: Fire—for energy.
Musical Note: *E*—for feeling.

DESTINY NUMBER 4

This orderly number agrees with your birth sign, Taurus. This doubles your patience and your endurance. You can go for long, long periods of placid acceptance of the way things are as long as there are not chaotic conditions surrounding you. Being devoted to your goal of making money (Taurians usually have this), or planning a home and family, you know where you are going and you also know how to get there.

The ruler of Taurus (Venus) brings devotion as well as love. You may know that you love someone but your intended may be unaware of it until you bring in the plans for "our house when we get married." How nice to be wrapped in the warmth of a devoted and loving mate! Who needs sparklers when your mate finally realizes the security of your loyal love.

NEGATIVE: **4** brings rigidity to a Taurian if he never lifts his head to see the bright sunny skies. He can become a plodder who is afraid to deviate from the norm and stay in his rut forever. If challenged he becomes argumentative and bullheaded, retiring to home ground or becoming hateful and suppressive. Stay away from negativity!

Number **4**

Color: Beautiful, healing green—project this color to people from your heart.
Element: Earth—the stable person.
Musical Note: *F*—for construction, building, making things strong.

DESTINY NUMBER 5

Taurus, the expanding creative mind vibration of the **5** brings change to original ideas that you may have had in the past. With this vibration you could take someone else's inventive ideas and change them slightly to make them better. This is the adventurous number which brings you out of your rut, brings you an exciting life of travel and viewing many new places. The changes can be physical or in your mental viewpoint.

This sensual number brings your Venus ruler into full sway over your emotions. Take hold of the variety that comes your way this lifetime; seize the novel and unusual. Famous Taurians like Salvador Dali, Orson Welles and William R. Hearst were not afraid to try different approaches to their work. Liberace exemplifies a **5** Taurus with his sly humor and variety of expressions. This worldly sophistication can be yours also as you develop your talents.

This also is the number of the greatest sales people. Use your definite, truthful and logical manner with your customers when explaining the merits of whatever you are selling. Sometimes your inherent brief approach or silence can convince others of your sincerity.

NEGATIVE: Monotony would affect your work or love affairs, Taurus. Unhappiness comes with too much drudgery as well as too much variety. It would be well to watch your inconsistency, your promises to do something at a certain time only to find that more interesting activities attract your attention.

Number **5**

Color: Turquoise—like a refreshing breeze.
Element: Air—the breath of life.
Musical Note: *G*—near the middle of the scale, denoting change.

DESTINY NUMBER 6

Your attention is concerned with home, family and mate during this lifetime, Taurus. Your family could encompass large groups as well as your immediate, private home life. Your steady, patient manner could assist many to find harmony in their life styles.

You have excellent judgement, and you evaluate situations with logic as long as you are not pushed into making snap decisions. Your sensible soul may take some time to analyze the situation as you deliberate in your careful way to find the best solution. This would make you an excellent counselor, as your quiet nature encourages confidences. As a teacher you would demand fair play, protecting the weaker students from harassments, yet bringing them to an understanding of their own self-worth.

Your home will contain elegant furnishings, not too cluttered, as this number prefers simplicity with quality and serenity.

Your mate or lover will recognize the warmth you bring to the relationship; it may not be as exciting as Aries, but your willingness to take responsibility creates a stable companionship that is long lasting.

NEGATIVE: The nurturing aspect of this number can turn into interference in the lives of your family if you try to govern them with smothering attention. Caring is not *carrying* the person on your back. Caring is the understanding and willingness to *share* your love—not overwhelming others with your tedious attention to unimportant details. Use the harmony of music in your meditations to raise yourself to the cosmic mother status.

Number **6**

Color: Royal blue—for stability. Meditate on this color.
Element: Earth—our planet, meaning responsibility to self and those around you. Getting "down to earth" with someone.
Musical Note: *A*—for receptivity, listen for the harmony or discord in self or others.

DESTINY NUMBER 7

This bridge from the known to the unknown could carry you through some mystical experiences during this lifetime. Think about yourself, where you have been and where you are going, Taurus? What do you want to do for the balance of this lifetime?

You could study the ancient mysteries or you could delve into a thorough study of philosophy. Whatever your endeavors they will concern analyzing theories to bring you more of the material things in life on one side or promoting better life styles for others, on the other.

Wisdom is the keyword, seeking hidden truths as you meditate on the metaphysical issues, deciding which path to take for further enlightenment.

Being a Taurian you will figure out what is best for you even though you want to remain free of mundane occupations. You are not afraid of the hard work involved, but you prefer to investigate before you leap into just any old job. Many scholars have this **7**, and with your tenacity you can travel far in this search for freedom.

You are the gentle lover in this number, wanting affection and sometimes rather undecided how to go about getting it.

NEGATIVE: This intelligent mind of **7** can get confused if pushed too far into concrete decisions. You would rather take as much time as needed to render a decision. If pushed too hard you might take the humiliation route and pull some downers on the ones who do not give you air and space.

Number **7**

Color: Violet—which stand for reverence. This lovely color can be sent for a distance for healing.
Element: Water—looking at your reflection and wondering what you are "mirroring."
Musical Note: *B*—for reflection.

DESTINY NUMBER 8

Here is where your stubbornness pays off, Taurus. Your need to have things your own way will bring you much material reward, providing you have laid a good foundation on which to build. This takes native shrewdness, education or abilities that you brought forward from a former lifetime—or all of the above—plus physical stamina. Eat your energy bars for you will be moving forward, building big businesses, corporations, organizations, or your own enterprises.

You radiate power in this number. Learn to operate wisely and make your efforts pay off; expand, capitalize and show a profit in whatever you undertake.

People will be impressed with your ambitions. You will attract many of the opposite sex; just whistle and they will come tumbling. Of course, we are talking about using this tremendous power to build and do things for the greater good with fairness. Don't grind down those who do not have your control and passion to strive ahead.

NEGATIVE: All this sounds great, Taurus! However, if you become the schemer, the con man/woman who works covertly to undermine his associates, you can fall harder and farther than the **4** who is just trying to get it all together. You are ready for big rewards and big pitfalls. Use your slower-going bull-headedness to avoid these pitfalls. Patience, patience to get where you want to get. Don't play the bigot, others have feelings too. Open your third eye to the beauty around you. Glory, fame, money and/or psychic enlightenment can be yours this lifetime if you use that wonderful Venus ruler power of love.

Number **8**

Color: Rose—the color of love.
Element: Earth—for achievement on this third dimension, this earth, material gain.
Musical Note: High C—for striving.

DESTINY NUMBER 9

Your love-life and emotional attachments may be intense but brief during this lifetime, Taurus, as you came in to serve mankind and free yourself from personal restrictions. This does not mean that you won't have any family life, it's just that your concerns over the human family as a whole will attract your attention more and more.

This number is brotherly love for your fellow man or woman, recognizing that everyone needs attention, needs to be listened to so that they can hear themselves complain or brag. Your patience is required in this number if you decide to become the empathetic counselor since people do tend to repeat the same mistakes over and over (ad nauseum) hoping for sympathy, not empathy. Your job should be to assist them to heal emotional experiences using the universal love principle.

Awareness and success, keywords to remember for **9**s, providing they do not possess others, combined with the vibrations of the Bull will assist you to continue on this chosen path of love (Venus).

Your chosen profession could be as a teacher, a psychologist, a personnel director or any occupation that requires contact with others.

NEGATIVE: Be sure of the facts before you charge ahead, Taurus. "Telling" your clients what to do can attach the responsibility to yourself, becoming the guru. If you do not want this role then find out what you really want, and what your clients really want, before exercising your tremendous power for good. Work through your Venus love and the **9** of brotherly love.

Number **9**

Color: Yellow-gold—for perfection, the desire to make everything perfect, even people.
Element: Fire—for warmth. People like to be around you, Taurus, for you inspire others to be more than they are.
Musical Note: High *D*—for accomplishment.

DESTINY NUMBER 11

This is the first MASTER NUMBER after all the single digits from **1** through **9**. All master numbers carry a responsibility for they are higher vibrations of the single digit to which they reduce; for example: 11 = 1 + 1 = **2.** So **11** should be written **11/2** to show that a person could be vibrating on either or both levels. This holds true for all the master numbers.

This is the number of the brilliant intuitive Taurian who wants perfection in all things. You also expect this in others, which may prove to be a little disappointing if you insist on faultless work from employees or those around you.

The impeccable behavior that you expect in yourself and others should be tempered with compassion. No one is perfect, yet we can strive for perfection realizing that each person has lived through his own experiences and has been affected by those experiences in one way or another.

This number has a genius quality, so there is a need to relate your mystical flashes of greatness to others as you light their path. This expansion of the creative mind is assisted by staying on the positive side of the number. Refer to page 38.

NEGATIVE: Your goals are so inspiring that your fame can overwhelm you and turn to greed and self-superiority. On the other hand you may feel that many people know what you know and then refuse to share your knowledge and insights because "everyone knows that!" A union with a **22** would be perfect if love is there.

Number **11**

Color: Silver—for attraction. You can magnetize other people to your support.
Element: Air—for the idealists of this world. The fantasies and air pictures you draw can become the realities of tomorrow.
Musical Note: High *E*—for magnetism.

DESTINY NUMBER 22

You already have the practical approach to most things that you do and this Master Number emphasizes this quality. Who can stop you now? No one. This is the number of the Physical Master, the one who can cure his own body of ills and learn healing arts to practice on others. Use your hands to send forth this Venus love and energy. Use touch, massage or some form of touching to relieve traumas of the body.

Rebirth through love brings success by manifesting order and loyalty to your surroundings, yourself, and to others.

You have an international direction, Taurus, in your work or profession. You can handle big companies, corporations, high government positions—anything or anywhere you can use your combined energies of practicality, honesty (even politicians need this), your ability to organize many people and directness (the Bull).

Your independent nature can set the goals, organize the business, get the work started and running more or less smoothly. Then step aside and watch the money roll in. Sounds good! There is definite power here to teach others your expertise and elevate them to positions of authority. Then sit back and govern.

NEGATIVE: If this vibration is too heady for you, Taurus, then the reduction to **4** still puts you in a managerial position. If your grandiose plans are just big talk, then you are negative. Get up and get going at your true level of ability.

Number **22**

Color: Red-gold—for practical wisdom. Use the things you have learned for practical purposes, not dreams.
Element: Water—for cleansing. Clean out the fantasies from your life and see reality.
Musical Note: High *F*—for physical mastery.

DESTINY NUMBER 33

This number brings softness to your personality, Taurus, because it tempers the Bull influence with tenderness and concern for others. This is your opportunity to learn how the emotions work, which emotions are minus and which are plus, i.e., which make you feel good and which make you feel yucky.

Emotions are a human trait. We react to situations according to our experiences and here is an opportunity to count to three, take a deep breath and discover just what is making you tick. There is an emotional healing in love when you project it to others, both for them and for yourself.

You can also think of **33** as being the combination of **11** and **22**—the idealist and the physical master (mastery over physical body)—leading to love and understanding of your fellow humans.

You are the highly emotional lover, or at least have the potential for this. If your mate fails to recognize you as the typical Taurus, deliberate and patient, when you surprise him/her with fantasies and exuberance, just let it be a mystery. And enjoy it!

NEGATIVE: You can fall into the trap of trying to control others through triggering their negative emotions, finding their buttons to push. A good thing to remember at this point is—when all this control is going on, who is the prisoner? Fortunately our present metaphysical knowledge contains information on what to do about "hate," "anger," "anxiety," and a lot of minus emotions which detract from the lovingness of life.

Number **33**

Color: Deep sky-blue—for intensity. Your feelings are on the surface and show in your actions.
Element: Water—for emotional mastery, flowing with or controlling the stream.
Musical Note: High G—for emotional healing.

DESTINY NUMBER 44

You might want to turn to page 18 to review the power structure in **8**, (**44** = 4 + 4 = **8**), the other vibration of **44**. All of **8**'s power and vision doubles for **44**, Taurus. Much material reward this lifetime.

This is the number of mental mastery, which means that you can school your mind to overcome as many obstacles as you want to. Think of **44** as being a double **22**—the practical master—the one who works with physical matter and things like building structures, instituting reforms in government, service, peace, prosperity and many of the fundamental objects and attitudes that affect our daily lives.

Another way to look at **44** is through the eyes of the idealist (**11**) and from this attaining emotional mastery over self (**33**). Remember that **33** approaches challenges through feeling. This emotional response brings a desired softness to you as a **44**, Taurus, for who wants to be a machine or robot?

NEGATIVE: An unbending, inflexible attitude will eventually produce a rigid person or personality. This is one of the traps of **44**. If you feel that you are always right, you could block out the assistance you might need in your job or in your union with your mate. It also could drive away your children. Mental cruelty is as bad or worse than physical cruelty as it continues long after a bruise would be healed. The scars are deep and hard to heal. Spread the emotion of love and understanding, listen to others. You don't have to take their advice—just listen—they might even be saying something valuable.

Number **44**

Color: Blue-green—for tranquility—the magic of speech as well as soft music.
Element: Earth—for mental mastery.
Musical Note: High *A*—for mental healing.

DESTINY NUMBER 55

This is the person, Taurus, who has abundant life, channeling from higher dimensions with ease to bring LIFE ENERGY into existence on this level of consciousness. Think of the **55** as being a combination of the **11** and **44**, the idealist connected to mental mastery of the mind. A **55** brings all the ideals through their logical nature, Taurus, and can bring their best visions of a perfect life to a sane and workable conclusion injecting the spirit (**55**) into all who surround them.

You can also think of **55** as a combination of **22** and **33**, which would define these vibrations as injecting the feeling and caring (**33**) into the life energy (**55**) by way of a practical (**22**) pathway.

55 is the life force that uses the energy to move into the light of knowledge. **55** acts as a prism, bringing the light and breaking it down into seven rainbow colors or rays. Each color has a different healing power and meaning.

When people come near you they will feel your serenity. You are easier to understand at **55**, Taurus, as your simplistic nature at this vibration brings all things within easy focus for others to comprehend.

NEGATIVE: Detracting life force from others is a no-no, Taurus. This would mean making others wrong, invalidating others' ideas, trying to be the ONLY force in existence who knows anything. This could mean mental cruelty, emotional suppression or scoffing at others' idealism. This is where the victims of life are still walking in darkness.

Number **55**

Color: Red-violet—for abundant life energy.
Element: Air—for spirituality. Discover the way of the masters. Meditate.
Musical Note: Chord of *G*—for spiritual healing.

DESTINY NUMBER 66

Use the Research and Discovery method, page 10 to see if this powerful Master Number is hidden in your birthdate, Taurus. **66** is love energy, the full realization that one cannot love others until he loves himself and can outpour this feeling to others.

66 is truly the cosmic mother vibration, the double six leading to the 9. $6 \times 6 = 36$. $3 + 6 = $ **9**, which is brotherly love for all mankind. We are not talking about sex, although that is an important part of lovingness, we are referring to the ecstasy that comes over us sometimes in meditation giving us the feeling that we are truly connected with the cosmos, the Oneness.

Your logical approach to life, Taurus, may not accept this version until you have thoroughly researched how this came about for you personally. This is not an ego trip; it is the full realization of the outpouring love through the acceptance of karma-free relationship in soul. You may have some more lessons to learn this lifetime about other things, but you have the love vibration to heal the gaps in another's soul at your fingertips.

NEGATIVE: Your logical and down to earth vibrations may get in the way of accepting this ecstasy as it may not seem entirely right for you. Why not you? Are you not worthy as a child of the Oneness to use this love vibration to heal others? Do not try to enslave another with your "love" or in the name of "love." Are you the leader who is selling others the idea that the only way to redemption is to follow you instead of your ideals?

Number **66**

Color: Ultra-rose—Meditation on this color will open the heart chakra more fully.

Element: Fire—for burning away the dross, the contempt, the frustration, the hate, and bringing forth the imprisoned love for self and others.

Musical Note: Any chord struck in harmony that brings you into balance, Taurus.

YOUR PERSONAL CHART

Birthdate MAY 18/1951 = 3
Birth Number 3
Birth Sign
Birth Element FIRE

This planetary aspect represents the moral excellence and goodness that the soul has achieved in former lifetimes, virtues which will assist a person in this lifetime.

Birth Musical Note E

Personal Year for 1988
Personal Year for 1989
Personal Year for 1990
Personal Year for 1991
Personal Year for 1992 8
Personal Year for 1993 9
Personal Year for 1994
Personal Year for 1995

2000 = 7

Personal Month Numbers:

January	9	July	6
February	1	August	7
March	2	September	8
April	3	October	9
May	4	November	1
June	5	December	2

Challenges: 5 9 7

Major 2
1st Sub-challenge 13=4
2nd Sub-challenge 2

PERSONAL YEAR

The PERSONAL YEAR NUMBER is the vibration that influences your life in any given year. This is a fine focus of JUPITER, the planet of benevolence and idealism. Jupiter showers you with all the good things in life as long as you recognize what the good things are. If you are operating on the negative side of Jupiter, it could lead you into extravagance and greediness.

To obtain this number you add your BIRTH *MONTH* and your BIRTH *DAY* to the year you are seeking. For example: if your birth *date* is April 26, 1932 and you want to find the PERSONAL YEAR for *1980*, do this:

Add 4 (April) to 26 (the *day*) to 1980 = 2010.
2010 = 2 + 0 + 1 + 0 = **3** the PERSONAL YEAR for the year 1980 for the person with the birth *date* of April 26, 1932.

Do *not* use your own *birth* year; use the year in which you wish to find your PERSONAL YEAR.

PERSONAL MONTH

Still under the influence of that great planet JUPITER, we also find our own PERSONAL MONTHS by adding our PERSONAL YEAR to the current month or the month you are seeking.

Example: April 26, 1932 is the birth *date*. We want to find the PERSONAL MONTH for *July of 1980*. Since we have already established the PERSONAL YEAR for this birth date for 1980 as **3**, we simply take the **3** and add it to the month of July, which is represented by **7**.

3 (PERSONAL YEAR) + **7**(July) = 10. 1 + 0 = **1**

Therefore, the Personal Month for the birth date of April 26, 1932 for July 1980 is **1.**

Compute your PERSONAL MONTHS and find the interpretations on the following pages.

TABLE OF PERSONAL MONTHS

JUPITER: EXPANSION, UNDERSTANDING, FRIENDLINESS, ABUNDANCE, INSPIRATION, INCREASE, SPUR.

The definitive words for Jupiter listed above captured the essence of the positive side of Jupiter's vibrations. Understand these words by using a good dictionary as you discover the true meaning for yourself. Meditating on all the descriptive words given in this booklet will assist you also.

The NEGATIVE side of the JUPITER vibration is: EXTRAVAGANCE, INDULGENCE, CYNICISM, GREED.

When we talk about the TIMING of your decisions we need to remember that Jupiter has an influence as well as the vibration of the number that you find for your own PERSONAL MONTH. The interpretations for personal months are as follows:

PERSONAL MONTH 1

Take charge of the direction in which you are moving. **1** always means creativity and being self-determined to take your own pathway, Taurus. This is not hard for you to do, for you move in a sure way toward your goals, maybe a little slower than some of the other signs, but you get there by persisting and enduring when other signs would have given up. This is the stubbornness of the Bull, using **1** as a creative factor to bring more light into your life. Be sure and check your Personal Year and Destiny Number with your Personal Month to see if they are compatible. Sometimes a number one month falls on a **2** Personal Year. This would only mean understanding that you can use your creativity, **1**, to cement relations in business or in your love life. **2** is the patient idealist.

NEGATIVE: Watch that your creativity does not take on the color of arrogance or bossiness. You could delude yourself into thinking that you were better than your co-workers or mate.

PERSONAL MONTH 2

Collect information which can further your plans for the future or the present. It's a time for rest and study. Small issues that usually would not bother you, Taurus, can be irritating during this period. It might be a good idea to delay any important decisions that have to do with conflict until next month. Peace should be maintained during this sensitive period. This is also a good time to look at your personal relationships, as a new union is possible. Your channels are open during this month, so you are sensitive to others' feelings and their reaction to you. Your friendliness does attract the opposite sex since you make the space so comfortable and beautiful. Check your Destiny Number to see how compatible this month is with **2**.

NEGATIVE: Because of the peacemaking qualities that this number brings, you are apt to vacillate in your decisions as you want to please everyone. This earthy constancy and devotion to detail may annoy your co-workers or your mate.

PERSONAL MONTH 3

Move forward this month, Taurus, with verve and confidence. There is more inspiration and fun in this month than there has been for a while. Don't coddle your mistakes of the past, just move onward—"today is the first day of the rest of your life." Express your talents in good company, parties, and interesting get-togethers where you have a good time and maybe even learn a little. On the job use your dynamic communicating skills in your charming way. See plays that appeal to your love of slapstick and broad humor. Experiment with exotic foods, candlelight and fine wines to excite the palate.

NEGATIVE: This is not the time to be intolerant of other people's choices. Don't gossip, no matter how juicy the information; you'll hate yourself in the morning. This would be against your true nature, Taurus.

PERSONAL MONTH 4

This is a good month to get your work in proper order, organize and categorize the different parts of your job. Sometimes you let things pile up, especially if you are a **1**, **3**, or **5** Destiny Number, since your ambition is to run ahead of the pack. Structure the different parts of your work, your life, and your emotional involvement. This may require discipline and dependability—you already have this in your Taurian nature—**4** influence is just an added impetus to getting your act together. You can also manifest what you want this month because you believe in your powers. Your clarity of thought prefers to see what you are getting into, rather than taking a chance.

NEGATIVE: There is a definite rigidity to **4** that can affect you this month, Taurus, if you are not aware of the exact nature of **4**. You could become so engrossed in your projects that you do not leave space for fun and lose sight of living your life.

PERSONAL MONTH 5

Now you can break out of the shell or stricture that the previous month brought, Taurus. If you used last month wisely, then you have a plan to work on and can be a little freer in expressing your ideas. This is also a good month for travel, for looking at the adventurous side of life and the interesting things you could be doing now. In business, you could use this outgoing vibration to listen to other viewpoints so you could accept that which is useful to your nature. This sensual number attracts the opposite sex, so take pleasure in the sights, sounds and feelings that arise at this time.

NEGATIVE: The variety that **5** brings to this month could make you restless and inconsistent. This is against your basic nature and could cause you a lot of frustration. Indulge yourself a little but do not overindulge to the point where your physical self loses too much of your stable energy. Relax, enjoy. Relax does not mean forgetting your innate poise and elegance.

PERSONAL MONTH 6

Assist your family and friends to find a loving relationship with you and with each other during this month, Taurus. Your almost unlimited patience can be focused on harmonious vibes with those around you. Your mate or lover needs extra attention now, and perhaps you also need extra loving attention. In business, use the best judgement you have to arrange matters to your liking. You can bring in higher knowledge by finding a quiet time for yourself to balance your energies. Self-realization comes through the love aspect of your ruler, Venus. Love yourself, feel yourself worthy. Evaluate the advice that will be given to you this month and don't be Bullish about it. A few minutes' reflection may bring the understanding that those around you love you and are trying to help.

NEGATIVE: You could be interfering in others' problems. Your anxiety about them could lead you into making careless remarks. Tread lightly in love.

PERSONAL MONTH 7

A good month for your analytical, refined and studious character, Taurus. All your columns must balance as you total up the year, your life, your friends, etc. No tag ends for you now. Your inner wisdom leads to better understanding of your fellow man or woman as your seeming aloofness melts a little and your graciousness appears. This could fool a lot of people and they might like to take advantage of your great good nature—not knowing that the Venus aspect can give way to the stubbornness of the Bull as you plant your heels down to get your own way again. Buy new and exciting clothes, do not be sloppy in your attire, who knows whom you might meet around the corner this month. **7** is the bridge from the known to the unknown, so cross over with care.

NEGATIVE: This could be a confusing month if you do not get your quiet time. You don't need to be a loner, just be alone once in a while. Friends whom you do not really trust may turn you into a skeptic for a while.

PERSONAL MONTH 8

An excellent money month for you, Taurus. Your will and determination will carry you far at this time. Rewards of material significance unrelated to money are coming your way during this month, providing you have laid the groundwork in the past. Sooner or later money comes to you, Taurus, and you can handle it very well. Esoterically this is a good month to re-open your third eye and experience the sensual side of your nature—smell the roses, enjoy the beautiful possessions you have accumulated, see good plays, visit art museums and let this aura of Venus take you "out of this world." Be prepared for emotional gains in love; a new experience; a new lover; or a renewal of an old one.

NEGATIVE: MONEY, POWER and LOVE could slip through your outstretched horns (the Bull) if you are not paying attention to this **8** month. It has power, and the Bull has a way of getting his own way, although sometimes it *is* by being thoughtful and giving.

PERSONAL MONTH 9

Since you generally have wonderful endurance, this would be a good month to clean your closets, pay your bills and finish at least some of the jobs you started several months ago. This is also a time to express your love for your mate with thoughtful gifts only you can think of, Taurus. That special bouquet of her favorite flowers or an interesting back rub for him. Your practical attitude needs order and cleanliness in your material life style. Also your mental attitude may need a cleansing, perhaps a little more outgoing friendliness when you are in a group. Many people respect and trust you, yet they may be afraid to upset you, so bend a little.

NEGATIVE: You could be turning inward at a time when friendship is all around you. Watch your inconsiderate or unkind words if your energy level is not up to par. This is not a time to be selfish or unforgiving if your patience has worn thin.

CHALLENGES OF LIFE

CHALLENGES are obstacles we encounter during this lifetime. We are now concerned with the timing of events that stop you from progressing until you understand just what the obstacle is and means.

In the FIRST HALF of your lifetime, you will encounter a SUB or minor challenge which is represented by a number.

In the SECOND HALF of your lifetime, you will encounter a SUB or minor challenge which is represented by a number.

The MAJOR CHALLENGE, also represented by a number, is with you your entire lifetime until you solve the mystery. We accepted these challenges when we decided to incarnate on this planet so that we can strengthen the weak links in our destiny. Recognizing these weak links by finding the negative influences of these numbers will be helpful.

SATURN is the planet known as the DISCIPLINARIAN, the teacher, the door to the initiation and all these good things we shy away from or fear. See Saturn's other side—if you have no game going, no challenge and life proceeds smoothly straight down the road with the same scenery—where is the spice? Understand the good that Saturn brings us. Saturn is connected to the challenges of life.

FIRST SUB CHALLENGE: Subtract the number of your birth MONTH from the number of your birth DAY or vice versa.

SECOND SUB CHALLENGE: Subtract the number of your birth DAY from your reduced birth YEAR or vice versa.

MAJOR CHALLENGE: Subtract the FIRST SUB CHALLENGE from the SECOND SUB CHALLENGE or vice versa. Place all these numbers in your PERSONAL CHART on page 26.

EXAMPLE:	May	12,	1951	
	5	3	7	
	2		4	= **2** is the First Sub Challenge
		2		**4** is the Second Sub Challenge
				2 is the Major Challenge

TABLE OF CHALLENGES

1—Many people will try to dominate and control your life. The remedy is choosing your own way without being belligerent about it. Know when you are right and please yourself after considering all the facts. Strengthen your self-determinism and be the daring, creative person you really are. Dependence on others can limit your talents.

2—Your feelings are uppermost and you are apt to turn others' opinions into personal affronts. This sensitivity can be very useful if you "tune" into people and see where they are. Cultivate a broader outlook on life and learn to be cooperative without being indecisive. Be thoughtful and consider the welfare of others as well as your own.

3—Social interaction frightens you and your reaction is to withdraw or become the loud overreactor. Each violent swing of the pendulum suggests that you are living in a personal construct without reality. Develop your sense of humor; try painting, dancing, writing or any artistic sort of self-expression that can bring out the real you.

4—This easy challenge is LAZINESS! However it can lead you into a rut where it is too much trouble to get out of that comfortable chair to answer the phone. Finish your cycles of activity and you will find your energy level rising. The other side of this challenge is rigidity. Learn patience and tolerance without becoming a slave.

5—This "freedom" number allows us to progress BUT it does not mean doing anything and everything we desire without paying attention to our responsibilities. There are laws of society and universe that tell us to use moderation, not overindulgence, in sex, drugs, alcohol or food. Organize your life. Recognize duties to family and friends.

6—This idealistic number may lead you into thinking that you have the best of all possible answers and belief systems. Your opinions can be dogmatic where personal relationships are at the crossroads. Do not impose your "perfection" on others. Give willingly of your time and knowledge without suppressing others' creativity. Turn "smug" into "hug."

7—This research and discovery number challenges you to become scientific and analytical. Heed your inner guidance. Develop a patience with existing conditions and make an effort to improve them. Do not stifle your spiritual nature. Your limitations are self-imposed. Cultivate faith in the justice of the general plan of things then seek to better it.

8—Wastefulness is the keyword for **8**. This can be brought about by carelessness or miserliness. A false sense of values, efficiency and judgements can become fetishes in the material world. Use your energies to cultivate good human relationships and avoid greed. Be guided by reason and not by avarice. Honor, glory, fame and money are okay if acquired in the right way.

9—This challenge is rare since it carries the lack of emotion and human compassion. It also means judging others and refusing to understand them because of an inflated ego. The time has come for this person to learn to love and empathize with others.

0—Here is NO or ALL challenges. Study all the NUMBERS above and see if you react to one. You have reached a point in your spiritual development where you can choose which challenge to release. Smooth the edges, learn and know the vibrations of the independence of **1**; the diplomat of **2**; the emotional thrust of **3**; the diligence of **4**; the expansion of **5**; the adjustment of **6**; the wisdom of **7**; the power of **8**; and the Universal Brotherhood of **9**.

If your CHALLENGES are the same as your DESTINY NUMBER, give it very close scrutiny.

NUMBERS

Every number can be expressed on three levels—POSITIVE—NEGATIVE—REPRESSIVE. This does not mean that a person is expressing on all three levels. You can evaluate yourself by observing:

1. How you react in certain situations.
2. What is your chronic emotional tone?
   Happy, grumpy, short-tempered, enthusiastic, fearful, bored, etc.?
3. Check how the interpretations listed below represent your over-all response to your daily grind.

POSITIVE	NEGATIVE	REPRESSIVE
Certain	Apathetic	Despotic
Enthusiastic	Unsure	Tyrannical
Definite	Antagonistic	Suppressive
Specific	Vacillating	Hostile
Searching	Non-feeling	Violent
Transforming	Covert	Stop Motions
Activating	Resentful	Hateful

This is the reason that people with the same numbers react differently to certain situations and differ in attitude towards themselves and others. You can choose which level you are now on and change your level if you wish to change yourself. You can also change your name or a few letters of your name to bring in the vibrations of your choice.

See our book on Name Analysis—POTENTIAL! This book gives you an in-depth analysis of your personality. It is soon to be available at book stores or can be ordered direct from the Rices.

Number **1**:
POSITIVE: Creative; optimistic; self-determined; creative mind through feeling; can reach a higher dimension of awareness when preceded by a **10**.
NEGATIVE: Indecisive; arrogant; fabricator.
REPRESSIVE: Tyrannical; hostile; ill-willed.

Number **2**:
POSITIVE: Sensitive; rhythmic; patient; a lover; restful; a peacemaker; skilled; responsive to emotional appeal with love; protective.
NEGATIVE: Impatient; cowardly, overly sensitive.
REPRESSIVE: Mischievous; self-deluded; hostile.

Number **3**:
POSITIVE: Communicative; entertaining; charming; can acquire knowledge from higher beings; inspirational; an intuitive counselor.
NEGATIVE: Conceited; exaggerating; dabbling but never really learning anything exactly; gossiping.
REPRESSIVE: Hypocritical; intolerant; jealous.

Number **4**:
POSITIVE: Organizer; devoted to duty; orderly; loyal; able to heal etheric body by magnetism; works on higher levels; endures.
NEGATIVE: Inflexible; plodder; penurious; stiff; clumsy; rigid; argumentative.
REPRESSIVE: Hateful; suppressive; gets even.

Number **5**:
POSITIVE: Adventurous; understanding; clever; knows the essence of life; creative mind on the mental level; traveler; creative healer.
NEGATIVE: Inconsistency; self-indulgence; sloppy; tasteless; inelegant.
REPRESSIVE: Perverted; afraid of change; indulgence in drink, food, dope; no sympathy.

Number **6**:
POSITIVE: Harmonious; good judgement; love of home and family; balance; cosmic mother; self-realization; the doorway to higher mind through harmony.
NEGATIVE: Anxious; interfering; careless.
REPRESSIVE: Cynical; nasty; domestic tyranny.

Number **7**:
POSITIVE: Analytical; refined; studious; capable of inner wisdom; symbolizes the bridge from the mundane to the esoteric; the mystic; able to heal spiritual gaps.

NEGATIVE: Confused; skeptical; humiliates others; aloof; a contender.
REPRESSIVE: Malicious; a cheat; suppressive to self and others.

Number **8**:
POSITIVE: Powerful; a leader; director; chief; dependable; primal energy; can open third eye; money maker; sees auras.
NEGATIVE: Intolerant; biased; scheming; love of power—fame—glory without humility; impatient.
REPRESSIVE: Bigoted; abusive; oppressive; unjust.

Number **9**:
POSITIVE: Compassionate; charitable; romantic; aware; involved with the brotherhood of man; successful; finisher; merciful; humane.
NEGATIVE: Selfish; unkind; scornful; stingy; unforgiving; indiscreet; inconsiderate.
REPRESSIVE: Bitter; morose; dissipated; immoral.

Number **11**: IDEALIST
POSITIVE: Idealistic; intuitive; cerebral; second sight; clairvoyant; perfection; spiritual; extrasensory perception; excellence; inner wisdom.
NEGATIVE: Fanatic; self-superiority; cynic; aimless; pragmatic; zealot.
REPRESSIVE: Dishonest; miserly; carnal; insolent.

Number **22**: PHYSICAL MASTERY
POSITIVE: Universal power on the physical level; financier; cultured person; international direction in government; physical mastery over self.
NEGATIVE: Inferiority complex; indifference; big talker—not doer; inflated ego.
REPRESSIVE: Evil; viciousness; crime on a large scale; black magic.

Number **33**: EMOTIONAL MASTERY
POSITIVE: The idealist with power to command or serve; leader who has emotions under control; constructive emotionally controlled ideas.
NEGATIVE: Erratic; useless; unemotional; not using his/her gifts of sensitivity to others.

REPRESSIVE: Power to work on other people's emotion to their detriment; riot leaders.

Number **44**: MENTAL MASTERY
POSITIVE: Universal builder with insight; can institute and assist world-wide reform for the good of mankind; can manifest his postulates.
NEGATIVE: Mental abilities used for confusion of worthwhile ideas; twists meanings of great statesmen and very able people for personal use.
REPRESSIVE: Crime through mental cruelty; uses mask of righteousness to do evil; psychotic.

Number **55**: LIFE ENERGY
POSITIVE: Abundant life; channels from higher dimensions with ease; brings light into existence; student of action; heals using life force.
NEGATIVE: Karma burdened with inaction on the right path; chooses to look backward and wallow in self-pity.
REPRESSIVE: Victim of life; in darkness; no path visible; withdraws; blames others.

Number **66**: LOVE ENERGY
POSITIVE: Self-realization through love; this love extends from self to others, knowing that one cannot love others unless one knows and recognizes the perfection of one's own soul.
NEGATIVE: Using love as a tool to enslave another; extreme selfishness and possessiveness; refusing love when time and person is correct.
REPRESSIVE: Seeing only the barriers to love; repressing loving attention to others; repressing the need to outpour cosmic love to others.

BIBLIOGRAPHY

Avery, K., *Numbers of Life*, Freeway Press
Bailey, A., *Esoteric Healing*, Lucis Pub. Co.
______,*From Intellect to Intuition*, Lucis Pub. Co.
______,*Initiation: Human and Solar*, Lucis Pub. Co.
______,*Letters on Occult Meditation*, Lucis Pub. Co.
______,*Problems of Humanity*, Lucis Pub. Co.
______,*Telepathy*, Lucis Pub. Co.
Campbell, F., *Your Days are Numbered*, Gateway
Diegel, P., *Reincarnation and You*, Prism Pubs.
Fitzgerald, A., *Numbers for Lovers*, Manor Books
Johnson, V., & Wommack, T., *Secrets of Numbers*, Samuel Weiser, Inc.
Jordan, J., *Romance in Your Life*, DeVorss & Co.
______,*Your Right ActionNumber*, DeVorss & Co.
Leek, S., *Magic of Numbers*, Collier-MacMillen, Pubs.
Long, M.F., *Growing into Light*, DeVorss & Co.
______,*Huna Code in Religions*, DeVorss & Co.
______,*Secret Science Behind Miracles*, DeVorss & Co.
______,*Secret Science at Work*, DeVorss & Co.
______,*Self Suggestion*, DeVorss & Co.
Lopez, V., *Numerology*, New American Library, Inc.
Rice, P. & V., *Potential! Name Analysis*, F.A.C.E.
______,*Timing*,F.A.C.E.
______,*Triadic Communication, F.A.C.E.*
______,*Thru the Numbers*, Samuel Weiser, Inc. (a series for each zodiac sign)
Roquemore, K.K. *It's All in Your Numbers*, Harper & Row
Schure, E., *Pythagoras and the Delphic Mysteries*, Welby, R., & Health Research
Street, H., Taylor, A., *Numerology, its Facts and Secrets*, Wilshire Book Co.
Thommen, G. S., *Is this your Day?*, Crown Publishing Co.